Six!

Ari Cueto

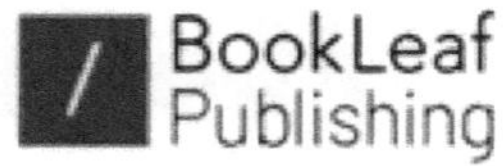

Presentation by *BookLeaf Publishing*

Web: www.bookleafpub.com

E-mail: info@bookleafpub.com

ISBN: 9789357210058

First edition 2022

DEDICATION

To Toby, for creating a musical that blends music and history in an amazing way.

To my mom, thanks for pushing me to finally publish something.

Family-Liz

My darling siblings, this book is for thee.
I hope you all understand why this is necessary.
Our father isn't a saint.
Nor is he the devil.
He lived a rollercoaster of a life.
One that was a bit disheveled.

Understand that this is our family history
but not our present.
We can learn from his mistakes.
And be more present.

It is with love that I wrote this.
It is with love that it was made.
It is with love I bid you adieu.

Here Lies Wait-Liz

Quiet was the night,
when the text was sent.
No call, no voice.
Just "He's dead."
Mary was a bit dry,
but that was her way.
Don't be mad at our sister,
She loved the mister.
Just didn't want to share.

I wish I could hold you both
and wrap you up in lies.
But our father is too well known,
Upon his grave, not many will cry.

So, here lies wait.
Our father, the Mister.
The one and only heir to a family of vipers.
Here lies wait,
a room fully of fakes and pretenders.
I pray I do right by you,
my siblings so tender.

But first, before I finish my part,
Let me introduce you to someone so far.

Heavy-Liz

Heavy is the head that wears the crown.
Heavy is the head that now sits down.
Heavy is the head sitting on the throne.
Heavy is the head in the unknown.
Heavy is the head that now grows cold
Heavy is the head,
here's his story unsaid.

The Paragon

Caring,carefree, and young,
Affectionate, assertive, loyal to your own.
This is who I was said,
Henry my closest friend.
Every smile, every laugh, every joke
Ruined by heartbreak and despair.
In the place of love is now bitterness
Never did I think,
Everything would be changing.

Wife #1-Liz

Catherine was an honest woman,
She knew Pops from way back when.
She is someone you can go to,
She is someone you can trust.

Her story with Pops isn't pretty.
In fact, her story is quite sad.
But instead of me telling you sillies.
I'll let her tell you instead

The Burden of Truth-Liz

Catherine wasn't suppose to be Pop's bride.
If it wasn't for Uncle Alex's death,
she would have never been by Pop's side.
Many thought Catherine was crazy,
For falling in love with one who is still a baby.
But Pop was a conniving young man.
He wanted her land.

But you should hear it from her mouth, not
mine.
The type of guy that just died.

Courtship-Catherine

A fly doesn't know where it's in a web,
Just chillin' being stuck in luxury.
Pretty words, flowers, talking at all hours.
Little did I know,
It was all an empty lie.

Empty was his promises,
Empty was his heart,
Empty was the life we were about to start.

Filled to the brim with such manure,
I can only hang my head and be demure.

Young and reckless, I became a wife.
Full of life and dreams, I was blinded by his lies.
Wanting so badly to be a wife,
I closed my eyes others demise.
Just wanted to be loved,
instead was someone he wanted to get rid of

Along Came Mary-Catherine

Isn't she lovely?
A beautiful newborn so happy and free.
Held by her godfather with so much love.
Her father missing , away on "business"
Her beautiful blond hair in little tuffs,
Her bright blue eyes barely opening up.
My baby girl, you are my light
Your father never knew what that was like.

Enough is Enough-Catherine

Cursed my spent youth,
Cursed my foolish pride.
Cursed the day I became your bride.
Curse the day we met.
Cursed the day I believe your lies.
Cursed be that my beloved is dead,
And in his stead you slid by.

Cursed be your lustful eyes,
Cursed by your wandering lies.
Curses that this poor babe's mum dead,
But in her stead, will I rest his head.

Cursed be those stupid girls,
Women that wanted the ride.
Knocked up and now abandoned,
Seven times you have lied.

Cursed be my weakness,
For yet you still seek my forgiveness.
Cursed be Duty's sense of humor,
I should have left sooner.

Final Straw-Catherine

Dodging you, she did
In fact, she just wanted your kid.
Very sure she was,
Of your raging love.
Reality check was needed,
Cheaters are always going to be cheating.
Even though I signed the papers, I get money,
the fame, and even the favors.

Wife #2-Liz

14 years down the drain,
Can't say that the old man didn't feel the pain.
Catherine took him to the cleaners,
When she found him with the housecleaner.
Had Mary go off to the Continent.
Boarding School stole away our older sister's
confidence.
Catherine took some time to rebuild her life
As she never was meant to be Pop's wife.

But in her place, came the worst of the batch,
She had a whole plan ready to hatch.
In Catherine's place came the temptress Ann

What can I say about my mother, the pain.
She is someone that I hope I can keep away.
Don't believe me?
I must be lying you say.
Let me read you a bit of what she had to say.

Daddy Said-Ann

Daddy said to butter him up.
Don't let him get the goods.
Wait until he's truly caught,
Play the lovesick fool.

Daddy said, don't fall in love,
Just sit there and be aloof,
Henry will come like a dog,
Woof, woof, woof

Daddy said act so surprised,
Horrified at the deed.
Little did he know,
It was all for his seed.

Daddy said you got him now,
Time to force his hand.
Marriage or your wealth,
Either way, we win instead.

The Unwanted-Ann

Push her out, push her out,
Get this thing out of me!
Pull her out, pull her out.
I couldn't wait for it to be seen.
Take her out, take her out.
I can't stand it anymore.
Clean her up, clean her up
Now show me the door.

The Plan-Ann

Crying, wailing, this babe is frustrating.
Sent for a nanny,
was looking for a granny.
But he hired the help,
This child was no welp.
So I see it in his eyes,
All his promises were really just lies.

Well, two can play it at this game.
Let's see how long until he's tame.
It's not like my looks are too plain.
His friends are not what they claim.

Looking for a new lover,
Needing to make sure I had the rubber.
Found one with a lot of green,
Time to leave the scene.

Oops I guess he found out,
Terrible liars all around.
But that's the brilliance of my scheme,
Found the perfect girl to take one for the team.
Got twins with so much potential,
Their birth was essential.

Another boy and girl to add to his collection.
A bonus, really, for my protection.
Well, there's my exit,
Enough your present.

The Truth-Liz

My dear little ones,
Not really little technically,
Your mom was a saint.
A real peach, take it from me.
Sure, your births were unexpected.
Much like mine,
yet, for you all, the stars aligned.

Pops divorced Catherine to marry Ann.
Found himself enthralled by her own plan.
Never did he realize that Ann was a viper,
She sooner poison him,
then let him get away with another happier.
Worse than the first divorce did Ann make his
life.
Though at least she left him to his new wife.

His True Love-Liz

I can not speak about Pops without telling you
about Mama Jane.
She was the best mom that heaven has ever
made.
She took me in along with Sara and Ben.
The three of us got a better mom in the end.
She was our teacher and our first biggest
believer.
Her kind heart is what made us all believe her.
She is up in heaven, that is for sure.
Watch over us forever more.

But to describe Pop's and Mama Jane's love
story,
I best bring in the one who knows it in all its
glory.

Mama Jane-Mary

Duped and heart harden,
The real Henry was hard to see.
His player ways left him with a bit of
uncertainty,
With many piraña waiting to feed.

Not knowing what to do,
He spent his time in a zoo
Where he found a lovely maiden,
One that unwittingly tamed him.

One whose heart was clean,
She was all that she seemed.
She sent him straight,
Didn't give him an inch for serious mistakes.
Power, money, and fame,
All meaningless for this dame.

Left to pursue her the normal way,
Jane Seymour was his heart's stay
The one he loved because she kept him on his
game.

Loyalty she demands,.
Loyalty he gave,

A family to love was what he craved.

Jane wasn't about the money to his name
She rather have him at home than in a rave
Jane kept him happy, loved and tamed.

Darkness APlenty-Liz

I was about 10 when Mama Jane was no more.
She went to sleep after giving Pops their child he
longed.
Pops was unstable after Mama's death for sure.
Had women coming in and out the door.
Mama's death hit us all hard.
Ben and Sara the worst.
She was all that they had after the divorce.
Their birth mom abandoned them, much like
mine.
And Pops neglected us as he was out of his
mind.

We struggled through our grief,
to be there for our new baby brother your older
siblings three.
Mary came to help a bit.
She was, I think, the hardest one hit.
Mama Jane was our heart and family glue.
Without her, we didn't know what to do.

Mary pulled some strings and got us a nanny.
Someone she met while solo traveling and
planning.

Anita was a bright spot in the middle of the
darkness,
She put up with Pops' harshness.

Wife #4-Liz

Anita ia an ally.
A friend and a confidant with no real need of
money.
She was more interested in her own honey.
She became our closest accomplice in schemes.
A big sister in all things that we would need.
She is the one you can go, she won't mislead.

Pops married her on paper,
but it was all vapor.
We just couldn't have Anita be deported,
So Pops figured he would get her sorted.
What's another marriage to him?
He was collecting them up like if they could
replace a limb.

But sadly, Pops couldn't keep his steady ways.
And Anita was not going to be shoved away.
Pops' cold heart made itself known,
And we all suffered its wrath without a groan

Wife#5-Liz

I want to preface this with this saying:
There's nothing worse than a woman that's
baiting.
Scarlet was not what she seemed.
Yet, somehow, the kids were the only ones that
could see.

Pops married the twit within a month,
Took him twice as long to try and get a refund.
The chick was older than me by five years.
I swear Pops had lost his marbles like his peers.

Midlife crisis or midlife despair,
I will never know.
But you lovely little ones came to be.
Shocking after all we weren't expecting three!

Wife #6-Liz

Marrying to help out became a theme for the
mister,
Though this time it was more for you three to
have a free sitter.
Katie is your guardian if you wish.
Though your siblings and some others are here
for you sis.

Katie was a business partner of an old friend.
She wanted her business to expanded
So here come the old mister,
looking for someone who was quite fitter,
to be his children's sitter.

Once Katie found out,
she wasn't a quitter.
She stayed with the old mister
until death came by in a whisper.